I Am the Night

♡ - Lisa
Kinser

I Am the Night

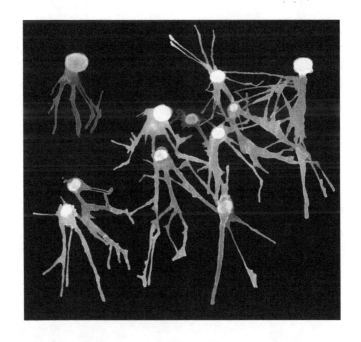

LISA KINSER

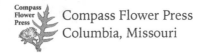
Compass Flower Press
Columbia, Missouri

Compass Flower Press
Columbia, Missouri

Library of Congress Control Number: 2023906140

ISBN: 978-1-951960-50-6

This book is dedicated to you,
and other people just like you.

"The hardest thing in this world is to live in it."

—Buffy Summers

This book was written over fifteen years mostly in the order you see it here. A sprinkling of current events, heartache, whining, blathering, and some hope as it all morphed inside me. The fifteen years I called My College Years, The Dark Years, The Shattered Years, The Brooding, Dancing, Dragging Years, The Loveless Crapper Years. It was, looking back on it, exactly what I would have wanted if my teenage heart knew what to ask for. It was dark, lonely, sad, exciting, addicting, social, full of fun with dear friends, and all too short.

I realize that I am in mourning for those years and in the process of figuring out who I am now and who I hope to be in the future. My party clothes no longer fit. My bars are mostly gone and my friends are married and now in bed by eleven. Fine by me, mostly, but I am nostalgic… John Hughes type nostalgic.

I find myself looking back more than forward and I fear that no longer serves me. My hope is that by finishing this book, I can turn the page and move on. I have to figure out how to let go and say goodbye. I do want to thank you all for being in my life and making all those nights out together so memorable.

Little Teddy Gone

There they sit a face in the crowd,
their little faces
they sit on the lap of Mom
Little Teddy Gone
She cries for her boy
lost to the storm
What will she do now
Little Teddy Gone
The Stuffed Friend
on my lap now
won't fill the space inside me
Little Teddy gone

4-23-95

Wednesday

Wednesday I lost myself
my heart, my soul
now on the shelf
out of my body
I feel no pain
I feel nothing, I am numb
Wednesday is over
but forever
I'll remember

4-23-95

Tomorrow I'll Cry

Today the sky is grey, raining
the sound fills the air
I feel a twinge in my soul
as they leave this place
we call home
home sweet home
Today the smells in the air
harshly drifting, biting
I hope tomorrow it will be over
only a dream
Tomorrow, I'll cry

National Day of Mourning April 23, 1995
Oklahoma City Bombing

Mommy

Mommy, my legs hurt
Where are you? I can't see
Ouch. Mommy, it hurts
I can't breathe
Mommy are you coming for me?
I am going home

4-23-1995

———

The Search

Man, where are you
Can you hear me
Hey, Can you hear me
Say something
You are going to be ok
Hey, Hey, wake up
You are going to be ok
Man, come on, Damn it
Reach out your hand
Come on, you can make it
Come on, Damn it
Come on
Shit-Why is this happening
Oh God, Help me

4-23-1995

Art

My paintings have faces, none like you have
ever seen at the shop or school
They look how I want not good or
bad, radiating mediocrity, sad

My words sound similar to the guy next door
who has lived and loved more
than I

My song goes flat at times, still I sing
trying to compete with Jones
denying my hatred for mediocrity
living it out loud without a voice
to sound like a song you have never
heard before or will again
till I come through

My dance uncontrolled and lanky
with promise of past lives discipline
and hope and will

My life different and similar to yours
but not ours, mine, you, me, us, what...
but it's still there for all to see
if you want

———

Red Lights and Smoke

On the bus facing you with the
Red light to create faith
what I depend on to show my face

We met here years ago in the
Red lights and smoke make all
the distance unreal

The Red lights and smoke make you love
that I can drink till I am full
but the time always comes

when the Red becomes white and
the smoke just burns the eyes that
wanted to see what you would be
if the fantasy never faded

———

Unborn

There was a time when you were mine
for awhile the house was home
the signs are there it won't last
maybe time, maybe love
maybe next time unborn

Before you were here things weren't good
the talk had stopped and most shot
in the path to beginning
The water seeps in and I choked
maybe time, maybe love
maybe next time my unborn

The gates of time have closed and we separate
you walk ahead, I will stay behind
maybe one time things worked
maybe love is worth
a shot
next time my unborn

For All the Ones I've loved

For all the ones I've loved
your charms melt the tears
your ways make the seas part for me
and I know that you don't love me
but still I love you so...too much

You all go I'll stay behind and bleed you
my fears keep me from you, your years
have passed I no longer have a chance

What I wish for most this time
to say what's in my soul
our love and time has grown till
you move on or I'll go but this
I know that it's all for
the ones I've loved

Zeus Love

funny games played to the age
of innocence, I wait for
you by the swings to come save me
and the time passes

funny games played to the age of
being young
hopes to a life of populous and praise
for all Mom and Dad said
was open to me
I wait for you by the car and you
pass by undetected, waiting for
you to save me and the time passes

funny games played to the age of grace
walk through the isles of denial
a few regrets — none loved or loving
of soul
I wait for you in the
hall with a ball in the mall
your Zeus love I wait for
I wait for you to save me
and the time passes, so I go on

Eyes Blind

Divas and Queens and the Popes delight
all Gods in someones eyes
not mine — but the hope of peace
all inside of me is clouded by
my eyes blind

Blind to the seas
Blind to the siege
Blind to me

All is well here where I dwell
motionless and still
waiting for the day to spread
my wings
Waiting for permission, a pass, a
truce, and order with no choice
waiting for the echo of sight
to open my eyes blind

Blind to the seas
Blind to the siege, even
Blind to me

Peace be with you
that's what they all say
dark as the night I sail with the stars
black as night I heal my scars

My lonely room a soft tomb
your call has long since passed
and yet the pain lasts
waiting till the day of number one
when fingers bleed to hear
what others can see and have seen
for quite some time

Peace be with you
when I come out of the shhhh — hell
of my own oblivion
imagined...

———

Fire's Glow

Things you can see in the fire's glow
all warm and moving to the beat of
a silent drum to which you always
march

Jump up supernatural and swirl
always moving speaking in phrases
no ears hear fully without peace
I was warmed there once that time or two

The floor changes with you near
and becomes a hole that swallows
me without a net to save whats left
when I fall

I can see things in the fire's glow
the heat hides the chill outside
with fuel for time restricted till you are gone

Jump up supernatural and swirl
always moving speaking in phrases
your ears never hear like the time I
was warmed there once in the fire's glow

Underground

The workers working with dark shovels
plowing their way through for us
up in the light — lifeless

Grubs work working with dark shovels
only for life and life only for them
without us up in the light for all who pass
underground

Dark and moist no sun, wind, cold
a mole, hole, eyes built for pain
with no shame to play in

I'll buy a shiny new shovel and meet
you where it's safe in concrete
tunnel to extend underground

That is where I will be till the threat passes
where people walk and breathe in light
where night is a passing phase

One Concert

I wait in the audience to see you glow
the rest are different from you and I
I think

Looking around as the smoke and sweat beats down
and the lights dim your shadow appears
for the first time for me

Pictures and words were past but
we are here now together at last
I will follow you till tomorrow then we part
I wonder about you, your words and mind

Are you happy at last or still lost without me
or you to find inside someone else
I think

One concert and a day later two, just to be
near you so far away in the dark with
the rest who are so different from you
and I

The road and time may part us but the heart of
mine will carry you till you come
back one day
for me,   I think

Norma Cee

Bones and skin hold you in — not well
hiding the scars you show to hide
your pain

Sunken face with big eyes full of life unfulfilled
unsatisfied, lied to like a child
beaten until you are gone from us

Your mechanical moves you hate more
than anyone else could know but me
my scars match yours that you show to hide
but I can't show mine

I make all this up from air to mouth to head
I know you like all do, what you want
you and Elvis — kings are dead inside from
social rot

Bigger that your head, more fight than fuck
contained in bones and skin that hold you in —
not well

Hiding the scars you show to hide your pain
but your eyes can't

Who Cares

Hide your face — we don't want to see
'cause you will see me fall
down like the rest of you below me

Why hide from what is to be — trapped in your house
with windows barred wanting only to go outside
and see the sun burn me like the rain

Me inside — who cares, not I, enough to pry
with the seed of love or hope or fate
I so want to grow with you

Playing hard — to get me — you won't
easy, not good enough for me or you
but who cares enough to try

Just remember cover your eyes so you don't see
how easy I could love you and push you
out of my heart for good — never for long

Dark Horses

dark horse like the ones in the
movies you've seen
getting shot — fall down for me
making my world empty and free

dark horses run through my heart
like the boys and their guns
getting shot — fall down for me
making me laugh at their stupid pain
so below that of God who sees me laugh
the cry at my hatred for me — fake, one, two, three

dark horses, running wild
ruining my mind full of shit and wind
stopping only to fall from grace and
make me wonder where I stand — if at all
misconceptions and myth
like the ones in the movies I pay to see
week after week
getting shot — fall down for me
or I for thee

Ones I've Loved, You Don't Know Me

In silence I loved you without knowledge
that I came
from far away to follow you anywhere
without direction
Behind you and quiet I watched you wishing
you would turn around and see me
without fear

The ones I've loved, You don't know me
I hardly know myself but I am here
and you are gone without knowing
that I loved you

Tomorrow you will see what I mean
as you follow her as she beats you
without knowledge
that I am still behind you watching
loving you as only the silent can

eyes closed
mouth closed
heart closed
for the living

Reflections

How can you look in a mirror
and dislike what you see
I say this to you and they
say this to me

Why do you love the unloved
and pray for impossible things
which comes at the price of lottery

I look in the mirror and dislike
what you see — that's not me, I say
look harder, deeper for truth, be

How can you look into the mirror
and dislike what you see
I see beauty, power, hope in you
and not me
I say this to you and you say this to me

———

You know, sometimes I think of you
Your smile I so seldom see
It moves me so and lights the
fire in my soul — your light is good

You know, those words, you know
you don't, we've never met when
eyes are open and mouths stay
closed for safety

You know, I know you — I think
our eyes hold the same grace sometimes
hidden by our face full of fear and
pain

You know, maybe time will smile on me
like you do in the night
when eyes are closed but minds aligned

You don't know but I do till the day
we meet I'll wait holding the paper
you need to read until you know

Moving around, travel, babble
Is it what I want or need to breathe,
I watch others collect lives or bits
to add to their collection
What I have is a huge chest full of
experience — waiting to happen

The key is moving, travel, babble, perhaps
only the first step will lead to the last
I want others to watch me and say
Is that how it can be to move and travel
with God's speed

Moving around, travel, babble
can only get you so far
if it's only in your head

I love you like that in a child's eye
looking up at me
I love you as the first blow of spring air
fills the lungs replacing stagnation
I love you through all your fears, your tears
that have long since dried
I loved you for lives gone past and still
I love you and I always will

Today at work I thought
about the readers who fill
their minds with other
peoples words
Can talk to each other about this
Quiet, I sit — no comment, perhaps stupid
I wonder if my noncompliance
is ignorance, laziness, lifelessness, dead
Or I wait to awaken my own voice
not to be content always listening
to your words from the past

———

I wonder what you think of me as
I smile, stare, look away
Next I ignore, leave without
saying goodbye, meet without saying hi
My stupid games hiding my need to know you
My stupid games hiding my need to know me
Only my words scare me more than my thoughts
Only one you can hear
But you can see me, my
outside doesn't match my inside
and I wonder what you think of me
then and now

———

I see that little girl standing on the
sidelines with tiny hands on the
fence, almost climbing
Come on out — you are up
The trembling starts and she panics
Strike one, shit
strike two, shit
strike three, shit
Back at the end watching, lost in
the hope of all dreams carried
drowning in physical pain
It will be her turn again soon
if the wounds heal for the trip
around to glory…someday
Heave me up to the top of shoulders

———

A hindu pyramid sits here
Move some bits around
Pretty easy so far it seems it
always has been for me
Times it gets harder at this point
So many other things to think about now
It probably isn't possible
How hard should I try really
It's just a game, isn't it?

This point always comes and I watch
Take a step back and sit down
Waiting for the game to say
I give up, you win — good job
It's about time, you have been a bitch
I knew I could wait longer than you
to be happy

This game is most patient and I grow tired
Of waiting — still so many other games to
play after this one. I'm bored, scared
I never get past this mountain bigger
In mind but a speed bump
I wait here for something to
push me over this crack in pavement
How hard should I try really
It's just a game, isn't it?

Have you ever heard of the perfect time
It's cool
It's when all the heavens and earth open up
when you become an angel whose bright
light shining
captivates the other so they are powerless
in awe, captivated by your beauty,
charm, sex, wit, intellect so as never
to turn away and laugh

Time, I hear stand still till you have said
All there is to say — of course so poetically
Then it slowly resumes normal speed
So the other is dazed and wonders what
miracles they just saw in you
And wonders how they never saw it before
how they could ever be apart from such
divinity

It's soo cool

Have you ever heard of this perfect time
I wait with you here until it comes
I'll be thinking of what to say
It's better to be prepared so when the
Perfect time comes, I'll work it right
To make all ends meet

Notes

Sometimes I am truly bored with my life
It seems there are so many things I
could be doing, places going, maybe whoring
for fun but I get up at 6:30 6:45
6:50 7:10 7:20 till I have got 10
minutes to dress 10 minutes to drive
to my slow job 20 minutes away

Walking in the exact amount of lateness
every day tail between my legs you should
know better you are 24 for Gods sake
Grow up and be responsible like everyone else
with their new degrees and unfulfilled dreams
Now they have got a one way ticket to
nowhere but with a paycheck enough to
buy beer and pot for the weekends when
the neighbors come over to wash away
the surrounding weeks

I went out with this guy last night
I've liked him over a year
Knee high to a grasshopper he is
Patienter than me and tall is he
So cute like a puppy ready for sex
He's smart and quiet
I want in his head
and bed to see how he'd love in the beginning
before it gets boring and too well rehearsed
his heart is pure and open, afraid
His eyes are whole
His smile doesn't fade in my mind like his age
It's nice maybe to be the first one he'd love
The girl who was maybe a fantasy — older, wiser
More experienced amazingly beautiful
Maybe he'd say that to someone someday
Real love he'd give away to a lucky girl
Someday probably far away — from me
He walks that walk of baggy pants
and tight abs, the kind you love to lay
your head on just to hear his heart
and breath till it filled my soul with
bubbles

5-13-99

The flowers on my grave
intact smell for a day but soon fade away
to dry shells of skin that blow away
when you whisper goodbye

Your breath overpowers their strength
to fight and they fall
like me into my everlasting darkness
without you

My hand moves up to reach for you
through the soil and I run for air
but I stop six feet too short
where you drop the last flowers
on my grave

Once like a butterfly's wing
perfect till the touch that
broke it all away
Now the wind blows through
my soul just to hear me
chime

———

In pale darkness you sit
Not smiling
Your black hair, clothes and soul
plead for me to know you
And I do

———

I once had a dream
that you were the bitter and I
was the sweet
In my mouth you sit
and I see that it's me who is
bitter and you are my treat
I'll have another

My Sunset

I'll wait for you to get together
and meet me on the path
to greatness
You forgot your shoes
I'll hold the train until the hues
of red, orange and yellow
turn black

———

Writing poetry is such a waste
A paper trail that others can read
when I am dead and say
wow, I had no idea she felt this way
I wish I could have paid more
attention to her when she was here
What was her name again — oh yea
Might have been

———

Just a reminder
I do have things to say
that you need to hear
They beat around in me like a
pinball game
racking up points as it bruises
My heart, my soul unfolds
Silver balls of will
running out of time
Do I have another quarter here anywhere

———

Today my pain comes in 6's
From all degrees, my heart and mind
Funny — I think of you and how nice
It would be to feel your hands on my back
as you kiss my forehead
and tell me it's ok
Of all the people it's you I call for
Maybe you'll answer
Maybe you'll let me cry to you till I'm done
Maybe you'll have to go
and leave me here as my pain doubles again

———

George

George died today (9-21-99)

He shook until we could have no more
Then his brilliant green eyes that once loved me
and looked to me for love, warmth and peace
will never see me again
Whatever follows
the shots, the broken heart, the pain
I would do it all to have you back
My little boy
My handsome young man
Rest in peace

As the week passes I may have one moment
of one day where I think I don't need you
or want you
That moment passes quickly as it lends itself
to complete admiration of who you are
My undeniable smile that always arises
when we meet.
If I touch you I could be lost
It will change it all — I think
That is why I stay away for now
But I can't much longer
I won't much longer unless you want me to
Tell me to go before we meet
And you will save me
from loving you

Your eyes have soul
that can't hide your thoughts
Your love, your fears even
if real you still scream out
your greatness. I can see past all that
to who you are and I'm pleased
Meet me here and let's
walk together — if you want

To my most desirable love
whose time has passed
With the touch of lips I could love you
And I do till the day my
breath falls short
I've used this line once before and here it goes
Forever in my heart you will be
forever dear to me

———

You say I should let my love
for you pass me by — not those words
exactly — but I can't think right now
perhaps as you move on to others more
easily related to yet not so true
as what we have and could have shared
just as in lifetimes past

Love another and continue to love still
It's what I'll do for you
But for me I'll think of the times
that I thought a different way due to
your influence, your strength, your patience
Your eyes that hold a thousand stars
as you turn them from me
continue to shine

10-4-99

I want to be the one who you will always remember
Perhaps the one true love that got away
Maybe you'll think — I wonder what could have been
I wonder where she is — I wonder if she
could love me still
In a boy's heart a bell rings true maybe expressed
outwardly nonetheless still rings
Please remember the sound your heart made
when you let yourself love me
and listen to my bell
for it still rings for you
It echos off the walls of the universe

My silence is filled with little floating hearts
and memories of events
of futures imagined
Your hands will be right there
within reach
but you pull them away
because I scare you
But you don't know what it's like for me
to love you
when I know you are out of reach
It was worth it though
right down to now
I look forward to the next time we meet

———

I kissed you one week ago tomorrow
You were still but willing
with my hand on you wherever it was
You touched me wherever you did
as we enjoyed each other
for a brief moment
A nod in agreement to meet again
sometime soon
I said bye and so did you
happily

———

The Silent Cowboy Singer

As I pull up to the yellow then red
I look over and see you
on your respective corner
that changes from day to day
maybe here or farther down the road
The music so real in your head
yet no actual words or sound is said
You sing and you dance for us
with your smile and beaten cowboy hat
in rain or shine
reminding you of times gone by
when your voice rang true
for more than just you
But to us you are the
silent cowboy singer

11-11-99

Weaving my web, weaving my web
Coming out on my own as a
full grown spider
sprouting my wings to set flight
above the trees up to where birds sing
I'm no longer afraid of the light
or the rain on the water spout
My web is strong and true
set to catch myself a piece of you

My friend Elvis
Costello? no fuckin' Presley
The king of convenience
of packaged sex and the American dream
Of a better day
when love and pain shine through
No longer behind bedroom doors
with whispers of discontent
The king, your moves rock my world
chasing my tail like a hound dog might

To a Long-Haired Stranger

I watch you ponder both
space and fantasy with your eyes
and that voice
of memories and desire
My heart races as I fight the need
to talk, to follow with eyes, to…to jump

You remind me of a soul
whom I long to meet
One far away or maybe it's
to meet you only
Your mind is sharp I'm sure
As your eyes and smile
I'll watch and wait for you
until science fiction becomes reality

What a world full of open dreams
open doors and open screams
of delight, of fear, of pain
all for one chance to be with you
as I uncover myself
one layer at a time

———

I came downtown to find you
only
That's why I came
I walked around to find you
only
That's why I walked
I saw you cross the street
with a friend
That's why I turned around
really
That's why I turned around
You went into the record store
That's why I walked some more
really
I walked around some more
to wait for you
I passed by the window and waved
to you
only you
That's who I waved to
What do I do now
I'm serious
What do I do

———

Poetry from a girl
you don't know
Why would my words mean a thing
to you
I wonder if you speak them too.
I'm the girl you see behind the counter
the girl you see bringing food, drinks
I'm the girl who answers the phone
I'm the girl who has ideas to change the world
and when I'm ready
I will
Watch for me

⸻

Once upon a time
I listened to a song by John Prine
I can't remember the words
the melody
I can't remember the rhyme
I bet if you played him now
I would never know
Yea, yea, I think that's,
Well, that's Joe?
You'll say that Prine is a poet
I'll say your are probably right
but I'd never know it

⸻

You may not know it
But I come to see you
mostly
As you sit at the door and collect
Your hat on backwards and
Fiery locks pulled back
You make a fine doorman
I'd pay money to see you
I also pass by at work to
Maybe make you smile but
Definitely to say hello
Your voice is full and confident
Your pocket chain dangles with pride
The memories you make clear
And share with the world but
What you should know is that
I mostly come to see you
You probably didn't know it.

I wanted to write a poem
that describes how I feel
I want to find a friend
who thinks I'm a big deal
I want to play a game
maybe spin a big wheel
I want to buy some things
or maybe I'll just steal

———

Meditation

Sitting still
my soul expands to fill
this room, this building, this city

Sitting still
my breathing slows, slows, almost stops
My mind is a sleeping lake
waiting for the morning geese to land
the fog rising and the temperature just so.
My soul is twinkling
for everyone to see
My soul is reaching
just to be with Thee

Sitting still
I go to my secret place
to wait for you to talk
or maybe we will just hold hands and smile
I'll stay for awhile
but I will have to come back

Sitting still
my soul awakens to a new day
of sunny breezes and sunny skies

Sitting still
I come back
as the tears gently leave my eyes

———

For Shattered

There is a place that I go to
It's dark and underground
A place with ballerinas and madmen
A place with white sound
I go there to see you
And fill my clothes with smoke
I go there to be you
A dark life with eyes of hope
It's a place where dreams may shatter
A place where life consumes
Down the stairs and into the night
To the darkness of my tomb

12-8-2000

I always get to the part
The time where we may become one
If only my fears were undone
Your life and mine
Meeting here in the street
I'll cross first if you will follow
If you don't I'll still come out
to meet you then come all the way
to the other side to see your back
as you move down
ahead of me

———

I remember one time you were sitting there
waiting for nothing but time
I stayed away
waiting for some kind of sign
I remember one time the hall
I passed by
You were quiet and alone
I wanted to ask you
before you went home
but I stayed away
waiting for some kind of sign
that I probably get
all the time

My weakness is you
My mind races for the first
dumb thing to say
My heart paces
for a chance to give some away

You are my weakness
Closest link to myself
You are my weakness
but my heart's up on the shelf

My strength is you
My heart races for the first
time I can love you
My mind is blank with desire

You are my strength
My hopes, my fears, my love
You are my strength
A gift inside from up above

———

You Theater Boys

Peace be with you
The actors
of life's plays so unreal
Once to experience fake love
fake emotion
in front of many
breaks my heart
that you are so close
and way too far away

———

When time is your passion
you are dried up and blowing
away from me
to a land of clocks and work
You misunderstand me
for I am not time
wasted
I can love you for one minute
if you will let me

———

All those things you think I ask
of you
are wrong
All I ask is for your eyes
when I am around
All I ask is for your heart
when you are down
All I ask if for peace
that I can find
by loving you

Rainbows and whispers
A cotton tail dream
All these things wait for me
All I can do is scream
I run away
Both night and day
from myself
All, all there is to give
to the wrong man

The funny thing about you
is that I never saw
or thought too much about
My eyes were focused on a
distant horizon, nearby
But then it was pointed out
that my eyes were unclear
and you had something
that I needed to hear
Now you have my ears
my attention almost entirely on you
What will you do now?
What will you do?

God bless the boys
whose hearts are true
Give them the strength
to do what they have to do
to do they have to know
to know they have to go
to that place where I sit
quietly
waiting
knowing that all they need
is probably in me
If their heart is true
perhaps I'll no longer be blue
or need new shoes
or look for clues
to life's mysteries
Blah blah

———

You silly cats
The games you play
Batting the ball
Getting tangled in the string
Why don't you just lie down
in the windowsill
together

———

My boys know maybe
that I need them daily
One to make my heart jump
the other I'll be ready for what?
I have to make a big move
to get my boys, I'll pick the first
because he is my light in
jaded armor
Maybe I'll pick number two
But his fire is being maintained
by kindling thrown by red
winds that mix and fold
to create a storm that breaks
hearts and minds
Is it blowing over or shall
it heal the land and leave it
fertile for love's crops

Well, finally you come along
and bring to my heart
a light that brings a tear
to my eye
And you stay away enough
to drive me crazy
And come by enough
to think that just maybe
I'll have a chance to love you
to feel a truth for a moment
at least until you change
your mind and turn to leave
Outside I sit alone and watch
the clouds cover the full moon
until darkness overtakes me

I woke up today and I missed you
I rolled around in my bed
trying to wash it away
but I am drowning
I had to leave my house because
it's too quiet and lonely
to be around others and smells
that comfort me
I miss you
It's too early to feel this
for someone who
will break my heart

———

I want you to know that this affects me
And I like it
I want to feel something
More than my own emotions
A reaction to yours
Or the others around
A new creative thought
Inspired by life

And so there I was
standing on the sidewalk
as you walk away
with her
Who knows what goes on
behind closed doors
after kisses on the dance floor
And there I was
one of the girls who groups to you
I am not
I was standing on the sidewalk
to see what you would do
And I did
These tests tell me what
I need to study yet
I have always gotten good grades
But anyway, there I was
standing on the sidewalk
watching you leave

Twisting willfully
my ebekanezer wit
Fuckish ties that bind my wrist
with black cord
Always returning to harbor
with an empty net

———————

The father has broken
after seeing my deeds
And now it is time for him
to play the games with young girls
in front of me
He thinks I played him
or was impatient or not a whore
when he wanted
But I was there waiting
for him to find the time
But no more
cheers

My drama is slow
and dutiful
like the good white witch
When all you want is darkness
with no guilt
It doesn't happen that way
for me

———

Sex is the tool for today
The more meaningless the better
How about a quick fuck
Then get out till next week
When we will meet again
At the expense of others

The process of waiting to see
what will happen
is passive and weak
The process of acting out
what you want to occur
is impossible
Impossible to be
without consent

———

Duck Duck Duck Goose

I rise from my spot in the circle
and I already know who I will choose
I go around patting people on the head
Duck duck duck duck
That one is too fast and will run me over
This one is too slow and I can't wait
There you sit over there hoping I pick you
and praying that I don't
so you won't have to touch me
or chase me or be afraid of the
reasons I picked you
Duck duck duck duck
You know I will let you catch me
I'll make it look hard
but you have already won
Duck duck duck goose!

As I sit here making a mockery
of my inner self
waiting for it to rescue me
as I continue to push it away
I realize
that I AM that I AM
Who is greater than the emotions I feel
Greater than the pain I fear
Only Truth is the objective
That I have tattooed and always forget
or push aside
for humanly pleasures
if they can be called that
The balance between what is and what can be
is simple
They are the same
until I stop twisting and manipulating them
into a shell of procrastination
I will feel no peace
The time is coming for me to grow
grow for myself not needing to wait
for inspiration
from others who spark me
But without oxygen I cannot ignite
I hold my breath
of eternal youth or novice
in a world that I have long since
received the key

I have often said
that with each person I see me
One thing that they represent
I learn from and take with me
I have often found
that I become very attracted
to the other for the lesson they have to offer
me
And I confuse my need to love them
for my need to love them
and miss some opportunities to teach
what I know
Because I get lost too
in the twinkle of an eye or smile that
cannot hide the true soul of each
that I always see much deeper than
even they can imagine
In you I reach a tough lesson
That I inevitably fail
for this very reason
I see in you a dreamer, full of passion
and thoughts that are almost too powerful
and overwhelming
I also see a little child with a giant
trunk on his back that he tries so hard to
carry
It is filled with rocks and dirt
It is filled with the fears
of the many who have come before
and continue to come even now

Next to the child is a woman
who walks along only to love him

She says:
beautiful one, put down the
chest and walk with me
it holds no value for you
you deserve all the world has
to offer you, only you need
to let go, no longer do you
need to punish yourself for
these forgotten sins that
never occurred

The child carries on
But for one moment he realizes that perhaps
she is right and considers forgiveness
But no, not yet
and he walks on
My lesson is this
And so is yours
In life many good things come along
only for you to have
sabotaging them for guilt
is unnecessary
and stupid

Possessor of all things good
Lover of all things fine
Reader of all things truth
Liver of all things dark
and meaningless

———

My eyes weep for you
And the emptiness you have
in your soul
I cannot accept
Because in order to fake kindness
and love
you still have to know what it is
maybe even felt it one day, for a moment
Yet you go along
not making excuses
faking life
saying it is just
the way you are

———

I don't understand your freaking appeal
Your looks are different
Your mind is sharp
Your heart is a breaking machine
That girls want and need to fix
But they get their apron strings
Caught in your gears
We get sucked into you
Then spit out the other side
With our heart broken
And no one here left to fix us

———

I saw your car
I knew it was yours
The black pit in my soul
opened up
I knew I would see you
and I did
Black pants, zippers, pocket chain
white shirt with blue sleeves
cut off
across the road
I was sucked into you, again
my night darkened
even before the sun went down

———

I have a hard time
looking in your eyes
My hope is that you will see
who I really am
and want me
and know I'm good
It also opens me up
to be broken
when your lack of awareness
can't see me
and walks away

I have a hard time
looking in your eyes
because you will love me
and I will turn you away
because you are too small
for me
and my blessed ego

I have a hard time
looking in your eyes
because I will see who you are
and I will love you

The seas will part
and I will fall
down from the heavens
to where you are
and I will be lost
And you will be nowhere around
to find me

I write all about you
making you immortal
Every move I take note of
and worship
as only a flower can
worship the sun

A book of poems
so everyone can see
you
in all your glory
Your death and disease
I glorify

Your worthlessness
has moved me
still

As I walk around
without a heart
even a beat
I see the sun shine
Then the clouds come
and overtake me
each time I try
to breathe

———

I miss myself
when I am gone
I don't recall
when I saw myself
last

———

Your thoughts are mine
sexual, hidden
Yours are on paper
now for the world to see
mine— in my head
Desperate for you to say
"Tell me about you"
with sincerity and timeless interest
This is the only way
you will get me
I stand here a silent follower
who wants to be your king
yet I bring no frankincense or myrrh
I have only myself
All for you or who I perceive
you to be
My lost soldier
One who can see my thoughts
through his eyes
One who lives my pain
that is visible to those
who have the eyes to see

———

I look into my crystal ball of deceit
I see visions of me
above your grave
thinking maybe I was the only one
who saw you
What about the three loves
whom you cut yourself for
Where are they
I wonder what they saw in you
Supposing they ever looked
If not
Missed the most beautiful sunset
Its colors so deep as to drench
My body with heat and regret
That vanishes eventually because
I know there are more sunsets to come

I think sunsets are a memorial
to a light that will soon pass
each one being uniquely beautiful
in its simplicity
only able to be created by God

I sit by the mountain
and watch the people pass by
reading the paper while driving
turning the music so loud to cover the
overbearing silence
Do they see me pointing?
Look over there — for it's passing
Before your eyes —time slipping
Assuming it even exists at all

Look at him and see
that he too shall pass
(just like difficult times)
And I will cry
filling my rainbow pot
of dreams to overflowing
proportions

———

At least I know that I was there
From the moment I realized
to the time when all color was gone
as darkness invites me
into the night of your absence

Moving towards nothing
a blind spot on my right side
where I think I see something
but only fills the space
between reality and mind

Moving towards nothing
faster than the speed of love
drug down by the
weight of fear

Moving towards nothing
that's what I'm doing
hoping you will be there
waiting for me

—————

The Night She Sat Up Waiting

He'd been gone three days now
She had seen him there still just hours before
her black dress hung limp on her
impoverished body

I stayed with her that first night
with her forgotten apron on, she acted
thirty years younger, making beds
watching the children
until he came home from work
so she could wait on him

I tried to tell her that he wouldn't be home tonight
A business meeting
Didn't you read the note he left, remember
the call he made to say don't worry
I'll be with you again soon

I pretend to be asleep in the back room
watching over her as she stood in
the doorway in her nightgown
Quickly ducking back into bed before
I was scolded for not sleeping
"You need rest at your age!" she'd say
"Tomorrow is a big day!"
(I already knew this and she had no idea)

He'd been gone for three days now
and each time she asked for him
we told her, he's gone
Each time she reacted as if it was her first
A business meeting helped
But she didn't recall a note
or a phone call where he said don't worry
I'll be with you again soon

So she spent that night waiting
in the doorway in her nightgown

7-24-99

Technology

There is my new phone
red, shiny, little keys
one light in the far corner
not blinking

There is my new phone
resting quietly, not ringing
not beeping, not vibrating
just still, dark, quiet

It screams a reminder
that you are not calling
not texting, not thinking
of me

I watch the little window
for a second of hope
of promise, of joy
but for now there is
nothing
just a new phone

———

My Life is Like Missouri

I am regular sized, have a regular shape, kinda square but not entirely. My look is kinda in the middle. Some people say I am a very beautiful state while others can't wait to move away from me.

I am as unique as any state if you are willing to read my pamphlets and spend some time. If you know me, you like me, hate me, or don't think of me at all. I can be overlooked by people who like California and New York, I am not blonde enough or hip enough to stand out much. I have a rich art scene that hasn't been featured in any magazine because I am not exactly looking for fame.

Lots of people pass through my life and think that the five minutes you spent looking around is enough to know who I am. You cut through my core, drive across my I-70 and then keep driving. You don't know me.

I have vast prairies, rolling hills and just the right size mountains. Lots of water that is filled with distorted fish and secret monsters. I may be in the middle but my life is solid. My foundation is rock although I do have caves that sometimes collapse and I am left with holes and scars but I am not built on landfill and illusions.

I have good friends, Iowa, Illinois, Kentucky, Tennessee, Arkansas, Oklahoma, Kansas and Nebraska. We are close but I still keep them arm's length away, visiting occasionally. I like having them near. My weather is extreme, too damn hot or too damn cold, too many cloudy days and not enough time to enjoy each season properly but I have seasons. They are unpredictable.

I need to see it to believe it, I don't care what the coasts tell me I should care about. I will wave to you in your car with one finger, depends on my mood which finger you will get. I have history and a future and maybe someday people will be able to find me on a map.

Dark and Heavy

It's a dark, heavy day. It's too cold and too grey again and it's making it hard to rise above it.

I am tired of disappointing people and myself. I am sad to even be disappointing my dog for not wanting to take him on a longer walk or stand outside so he can roll around in the grass and eat sticks.

I want to build my life the way I want it. It's not the way others may want me to and it's not the most stable way at this point but I have to. If I don't I will die. My soul. My soul will die. What a drama queen. Why don't you just get a job. I have a job. Why don't you just do what you are supposed to do. I can't do it all. I believe life is to be an adventure but what does that even mean.

I am dark and heavy today. Time to start drinking. I want to do something so that after I am gone there will be something left that proves I was here. I have to find that thing and build it because they haven't dropped it off at my house yet with a big red bow on it. I know it is out there, I have felt it. I can feel it again. Happiness. What can I do for you but show you that you can feel it too. Even if you are having a dark and heavy day yourself.

Today I feel like I am near the edge and I may fall over. I have felt this many times and it always works out. It always does but right now I may break. Who can I turn to to listen to my tale who isn't so weighed down with their own? The darkness is a lie and the light is a dream. I am a dreamer and I will keeping fighting, rising above it, just to go outside and take a walk. I need a sunny day and good food. I need you to be ok. I want to know I am on the right path and that things will be ok and I won't have to give up...on myself. I can do without a lot to make time for what I want to have. Peace. Hope. Light. I know I can feel it but how long will it last next time. Will I lose myself on the next cloudy day? I want you to know that I am here for you. Being here for you gives me a reason to be. Be.

I am dark and heavy right now. Tomorrow will be better.

Death

All I saw was my friend with a gun in his hand. I knew it was going to happen and that he was going to do it because he was my friend. If not him, right then, it was going to be the other. I closed my eyes and put my fingers in my ears so I wouldn't hear the gun go off. I waited for the impact on my head. I wondered how quick it would be. I didn't hear anything. After awhile I opened my eyes to see if he had changed his mind. Everything looked the same, maybe quieter. Time felt different. I was walking around and no one was really looking at me. That's was okay, I was used to that. I think, maybe my friend hadn't changed his mind.

I noticed that I could go wherever I thought about. I was in an office building, people were working and they were having a carry in. I wondered if I could eat anything. I know I didn't need to eat anything but could I? I put a piece of cookie in my mouth. I could feel a texture but mostly air. The slightest hint of the flavor that I once knew so well. I don't know why but I took my top off. Finally free because no one can see me and I can still feel the sunlight on what used to be my skin. Actually, some people can see me and the first time I knew she could I covered up my ghostly presence and blushed with a rosy glow. I guess if I was to be out and about, I would wear clothes. Dang, and I thought this was Heaven.

I asked some of the others how things worked here. It was almost the same as it worked there only faster. Think of something and it appears. That would have been nice on the heavier plane but that was not the point of it. I wondered if Wally was around. Instantly, he came into the room and was talking to a lady over in the corner. I didn't see his face when he came in but he had the same haircut. He did adjust his height and was a little taller and he looked older, wiser. He came over to me and we hugged. It felt like a real hug. Substance. He told me he had been here nineteen years, like he had moved and was really enjoying the place. Nineteen years? Had it really been that long, seemed like just yesterday. I said, "Hey Wally, can we actually see our pets over here?" He looked down at the ground and there was fuzzy brown dog running around his feet. I asked to see my Buddy. The next instant he was there and in my arms. He had adjusted his facial hair and it had more curls under his chin but he was still beautifully white and smiling! "It is so nice to see you again, my friend!" I think I can get to like it here.

About the Author

Lisa Kinser is a writer, poet, and educator. She is also an Integrative Nutrition and LifeStyle Coach and End of Life Planner. www.LisaKinser.com

She has enjoyed (on occasion) riding motorcycles, paranormal investigating, traveling, and skydiving.

Ms. Kinser lives on her family farm with her husband, Luke, their dogs, cats, chickens, ducks, and guineas.

Printed in the USA
CPSIA information can be obtained
at www.ICGtesting.com
JSHW020949270923
48968JS00004B/20

9 781951 960506